# HEALING THE
# WOUNDS OF
# EMOTIONAL
# ABUSE

# HEALING THE WOUNDS OF EMOTIONAL ABUSE

## The Journey Worth The Risk

NANCY BENVENGA

**Resurrection Press**
Mineola · New York

First published in February, 1996 by Resurrection Press, Ltd.
P.O. Box 248
Williston Park, NY 11596

Second printing – July, 1997

ISBN 1-878718-30-4

Library of Congress Catalog Card Number 95-72648

Cover design by John Murello
Author picture by Anton de Flon

Printed in the United States of America.

*To my dear friends*
*Msgr. Jim Lisante*
*and Dr. Eileen McKeown*
*with much love and gratitude*

# Contents

PREFACE                                          9

1. AN INTRODUCTION TO THE PROBLEM                11

2. NO ONE DESERVES ABUSE                         32

3. THE LEGACY OF ABUSE                           47

4. HEALING: THE JOURNEY WORTH THE RISK           61

5. MEDITATIONS AND PRAYERS                       76

6. RESOURCES                                     86

# Preface

"I'm here to ensure that you don't end up forming the kind of home I grew up in!"

That is what I tell the engaged couples to whom I give Abuse and Addiction talks as part of their marriage preparation in the Catholic pre-Cana program. For many of us, in one sense, it's too late: we have already grown up in "that kind of home" and we have the psychic wounds to prove it. But in another sense, it's never too late: never too late to undertake the journey that will heal us from these wounds and lead us to a new life free of the distortions we absorbed in childhood; never too late to examine our own attitudes toward parenting — another legacy of our childhood — and take the steps necessary so that when we become parents we do not perpetuate the abusive behavior we learned in our families of origin; never too late, if we are teachers or other professionals, to learn to recognize the signs of emotional abuse in the children in our care so that we may bring about intervention and assistance for these families at risk.

Physical and sexual abuse are much in the media. Why, you may wonder, do I choose to write about emotional abuse?

For one thing, precisely because it is the "forgotten" form of abuse. It leaves no graphic evidence — no broken bones, no ugly bruises — to betray its existence. Yet emotional abuse can go on undetected for years, wearing away and even crushing the spirit of its victims; and, if unacknowledged and unhealed, it will carry on to the next generation as the abused becomes the abuser in a tragic, vicious cycle.

For another thing, emotional abuse is the kind of abuse that I experienced. Many of the illustrations of abusive situations included in this book are from my own life. If the Lord has given me a "well-trained tongue" (well-trained pen?), I intend to use that gift to help others like myself as well as those who want to stop the cycle of abuse in their own families and in the families with whom they come into contact pastorally and professionally. As I said at the beginning, I'm here to help ensure that the kind of family I grew up in soon becomes a relic of the past.

There are several people I would like to thank for their support, encouragement and inspiration. They include, above all, my two friends and mentors to whom this book is dedicated, Dr. Eileen McKeown and Msgr. Jim Lisante; my great friend and editor Emilie Cerar; and my own "gifted sculptor," Fr. Anthony Doe of Westminster, England. Also, Fr. Peter Vaccari, Sr. Mary V. Maher, Pat Mosunic, Fr. John Dillon, my son Anton, who has the makings of an insightful spiritual guru — and his father, with whom I am still great friends.

*Long Island, August 1995*

# 1

# An Introduction to the Problem

I was an aesthetically challenged child. Or so I thought. Actually, in those days before politically correct language became the rage, the term was "ugly." "You're an ugly child!" — that was my mother's favorite epithet for me, and the hatred that twisted her face whenever she hurled it out left no doubt in my mind that my alleged ugliness, far from being merely "skin deep," permeated my entire being and rendered me quite unworthy of love.

I was also a "disposable" child — and this in an era that predated our throw-away society by many years. My mother would threaten to get rid of me at the slightest provocation. She relished intimidating me with images of an establishment called the "Pig Pen," a place of indescribable filth and chaos to which people who sinned against the virtue of tidiness were sent and condemned to live out their days. If, for example, I left some toys in the living room she not only threatened to send me to the Pig Pen but even, on at least one terrifying occasion, actually went through the motions of telephoning and arranging for "them" to come and get me.

It doesn't take long for this sort of treatment to have noticeable effects on a child. By age five I had perceived the world to be a place that didn't want me. On my first day of kindergarten, while the other children were happily playing in the groups they had casually formed, I cowered alone in a corner, afraid to approach anyone. The teacher eventually took me by the hand and introduced me into a group of children; later, my mother told me that Sister Mary Albert had commented that I would "never be a leader."

To this kindergarten pupil a "leader" was the lucky child who got to be first in line and lead the class out of school, for recess or at the end of the day. Sister had promised us that we would each get our turn to be leader some time during the year. Now I was hearing (for so I interpreted it) that my turn would never come. The privilege that each child in the class would enjoy at some point would never be mine.

Sister Mary Albert, of course, was making a prediction not about my place in the class line but about my future character development — a prediction that, as it turned out, had as much basis in truth as did my mother's opinion of my looks.

*Today, I hope, a kindergarten teacher observing a frightened child cowering in a corner will not draw a conclusion about an inborn personality trait but will instead recognize the signs of an insidious process of emotional abuse.*

## A Picture of Child Abuse

The so-called "battered child syndrome" was first recognized by the medical profession in 1961. Initially the term referred to serious nonaccidental physical injury, but now the concept of "child abuse" also includes sexual and emotional abuse and neglect. My experience began some years before a name existed for it and, obviously, before statistics were kept for it. Current statistics paint a frightening picture of the reality of child abuse today:

- 3.1 million children in America suffer physical, emotional or sexual abuse or neglect each year.

- One child out of four experiences abuse at some time.

- No one social or economic class or ethnic background has a monopoly on child abuse: it exists across the board, in white homes as well as black, rich as well as poor, among the professional as well as the working classes.

- In 85 percent of cases the abuser is someone whom the child knows and trusts.

- More than three children die in the U.S.A. each day from abuse or neglect.

In our society, physical and sexual abuse receive the most attention. Their effects are dramatic and graphic: Who can forget the haunted face of Lisa Steinberg, cruelly battered until she died of her injuries? Who doesn't cringe in pain at newspaper reports of babies being thrown against a wall by the mother's boyfriend or being seared with cigarette burns by the mother herself? But emotional abuse is no less destructive, no less important to watch for. Compared with physical or sexual abuse, the detection of emotional abuse is not straightforward. Its effects are intangible, its evidence usually not concrete enough for a report to be made to the authorities: No black eye screams for attention, no broken bone awakens suspicion. Yet the wounds inflicted by emotional abuse are often deeper, for the abuse itself, in the absence of physical evidence to draw attention to it and bring it to a halt, often lasts longer than physical abuse. "A broken bone shows up on an X-ray, but emotional harm often is invisible."[1]

## Definition, Types, Signs

The National Center on Child Abuse and Neglect defines psychological and emotional abuse as

> child abuse which results in impaired psychological growth and development. Frequently occurs as verbal abuse or excessive demands on a child's performance and results in a negative self-

image on the part of the child and disturbed child behavior. May occur with or without physical abuse.[2]

Emotional abuse can include:

- *chronic ridicule* of a child's looks, abilities, fears, ideas, accomplishments;

- *scapegoating* or blaming a child without cause;

- *terrorizing* by, for example, threatening to beat or abandon the child; repeatedly yelling at the child;

- letting the child witness scenes of family violence;

- *punishing a child for normal behavior* (for example, running, smiling);

- *rejecting a child* through, for example, cruel remarks ("You're an ugly child!") or obviously favoring a sibling;

- *ignoring* or *isolating* the child;

- *humiliating* the child.

The concept of *competence* has become important in assessing the possibility and extent of emotional abuse of children. According to psychologist David McClelland, competence "involves successful performance in specific social contexts that include communication skills, patience, moderate goal setting, and ego development."[3] Competence is the quality that empowers the human person to function as a harmonious and productive member of society; it is the goal of effective childrearing, the outcome of effective caring. Emotional abuse seriously impairs the development of competence in a child; thus, the process of competence development can be observed in any given child in order to evaluate the emotional quality of the caregiving that the child is receiving.

To be alert to the signs of emotional abuse, adults (teachers, for example) need to observe the behavior of parents as well as children. Two general clues should arouse concern:

1. *in the child*, impaired emotional development and ability to function in social relationships: for example, low self-esteem, inappropriate responses to normal adult behavior.

2. *in the parent*, any evidence of inappropriate or inadequate care for the child's emotional health, especially any treatment that seems to go against common sense.

*If a child:*

- displays aggressive or hostile behavior

- is withdrawn and overly shy

- seems depressed

- does poorly in school

- consistently allows him- or herself to be dominated by others

*If a parent:*

- belittles the child or yells at the child in public

- abuses alcohol or other substances

- never seems satisfied with the child's achievements

- is isolated from the community and refuses to meet with school authorities

- punishes the child for normal behavior, such as smiling

— then the possibility of emotional abuse should be considered. The presence of such clues should be a warning, not to jump immediately to conclusions, but to observe the child and its family more closely. My own motto: *Look beyond appearances!*

A teacher may think it's a great blessing to have an angelic child in the class, but the child who is "too good to be true" is quite possibly being abused at home and is therefore afraid to risk taking even the slightest step out of line for fear of major retaliation. After repeatedly being threatened or punished for the slightest thing, I was quite afraid of my own shadow by the time I started school. Meeting adults in the street — for example, neighbors or my friends' mothers — and having to say hello to them was torture. One time — I may have been nine or ten — I was standing outside the building where I lived when a couple of girlfriends passed by and greeted me. Before I could open my mouth the mother of one of the girls, who was bringing up the rear, said to them, "Don't say hello to her, she never says hello to anyone."

*In that less enlightened time this woman proba-bly just assumed that I was a rude child. I hope that today an adult observing that a certain child "never says hello" will be alert to the possibility that the parents are abusing the child.*

When I was in the first grade, the teacher asked us to explain to the class what we wanted to be when we grew up and why. I said that I wanted to be a teacher. But my motivation had nothing to do with imparting knowledge; instead I concentrated on de-scribing the dreadful punishments I would mete out to misbehaving pupils, including keeping them at school all night. Given my frame of reference, molded by the drastic punishments I experienced or was threatened with, such punitive action would have seemed quite normal to me.

*The teacher let me finish speaking and then went on to the next child. I hope that today such a display of a vindictive attitude on the part of a six-year-old will cause the teacher to suspect unusually harsh treatment in the child's home.*

While I was a withdrawn, frightened little girl who lived out my aggressions in fantasies such as the above, an abused child may also react at the other ex-treme, acting belligerent and bullying other children. The difference lies in the child's inborn temperament. A boy named Ricky in our neighborhood was a loudmouthed bully, one of the oldest children on the block who was never happy unless he had organized all the other kids and was ordering them around, keeping them "in line" with a repertoire of well-chosen insults. The adults in the neighborhood couldn't understand how such "nice," respectable parents could have had a son like Ricky. The clue was obvious, had anyone cared to read it. Ricky was very polite, almost overly polite, to adults, in a way that suggested not phoniness but fearful respect. Kept firmly under the thumb of his "nice" parents, Ricky took out his aggressions on children younger than himself.

*I hope that today adults confronted with the Rickies in their neighborhoods will look beyond appearances and question what life is really like for Ricky in his "nice" parents' home.*

It is vitally important for adults who come into close contact with children (teachers, clergy, medical personnel, for example) to become familiar with the indications of possible emotional abuse. Why?

(a) Children do not come and tell you they are being abused. The younger ones haven't even the vocabulary.

(b) Most children are protective of even the most toxic parents, possibly out of fear of being taken from them; this, after all, is the only home they know.

(c) Not knowing any better, they think the situation is normal; they assume that all homes are like theirs.

(d) They believe that they deserve the treatment they are getting. A parent's frame of reference is the only basis the child has for his or her self-worth: If a mother calls her daughter ugly, it must be true, because the parent said so. If a father tells his son that he will never amount to anything, it must be the truth: the parent knows everything.

As I've already mentioned, it is not as easy to detect emotional abuse as it is to discover physical abuse. Emotional abuse does not present concrete, conclusive evidence such as a broken bone or discolored eye.

Certain categories of persons are "mandated" or required to report suspected cases of child abuse. Those categories differ from state to state, but they always include teachers and other school personnel and can also include physicians, social services workers and others who come into contact with children through health, pastoral or legal services.[4] Even if you do not fall into a mandated category, remember that reaching out to the authorities in this way could change a young person's life. Only the *suspicion* need exist — you will not be asked for hard evidence — and your confidentiality will be respected. Each state has its own reporting hotline; please see the Resources in chapter 6 under "Hotline."

## Neglect: A Sin of Omission

*Abuse* is what a parent *does*. When a parent does *not* do what she *ought* to do, on the other hand, this constitutes *neglect*. Neglect is a sin not of *com*mission but of omission. The neglectful parent does *not* show affection, does *not* spend time with the child, does *not* provide for basic nutritional, medical or hygienic needs. Neglect is really a form of abuse — over 90 percent of reported cases of child abuse in New York are cases of neglect.

Neglect, like abuse, can fall into different categories. Physical and medical neglect, as well as abandonment, are obvious. Emotional neglect, like emotional abuse, is the most difficult to identify. "Generally, it consists of the failure to provide emotional support to children in ways that are appropriate for the age and development of the child"[5] and includes failure to obtain necessary mental health services and to share and display feelings. Emotional neglect can exist quite independently of physical neglect: some children have every material need provided for, yet their emotional needs — for affection, affirmation, guidance and proper discipline — are woefully overlooked. When they turn out to be deeply troubled and bitter young people, the parents cannot understand what went wrong — after all, they have been "good providers"!

Neglect shares with emotional abuse the quality of being *chronic* — by its very nature it never consists of an isolated incident but takes place over an extended period of time. The harm from neglect "results, like the wearing away of stone by the constant drip of water, from the accumulated effect of numerous opportunities for action which do not occur."[6]

Chronic emotional neglect can affect the child's development in a number of ways, resulting in low self-esteem, poor interpersonal relationships and limited motivation.

"Emotional orphans" is an apt term for children who suffer from emotional neglect. There actually are young people who enjoy an otherwise comfortable living standard but whose parents have never hugged them or told them they love them! In most cases such parents never display affection toward each other either, so that the children grow up abnormally reserved and incapable of either giving or receiving love.

When I was thirteen I went one Sunday to call for my friend Marion. We planned to spend the afternoon at the United Nations Building in New York City. As we left her apartment Marion and her mother kissed each other goodbye. "Oh!" I thought. "So parents and children do that!" It was a revelation to me. It must have been at the age of five or six that I had formulated the essence of the relationship between parents and children to be something like this: "Parents order children around and the children have to obey, otherwise they get punished." Small wonder that many years later a close male friend told me, "You don't know how to be loved."

## Alcohol: Toxic Accomplice

Emotional orphanhood is especially likely to exist when addiction and codependency are present. The alcoholic parent is too involved with her addiction to be aware of the child's needs. The codependent parent, meanwhile, is burdened by the demands of the alcoholic parent and is so wrapped up in his identity as the addict's "caretaker" that he, too, becomes oblivious to the child's emotional needs.

My friend Valerie lived with her father, her mother — an emotionally abusive, suicidal alcoholic — and her younger brother, Bobby. Just around the time Valerie entered college and Bobby began high school, the mother's alcoholism and emotional instability escalated to an intolerable degree — intolerable, at least, for Valerie and Bobby. Valerie began suffering from anorexia — not the much publicized kind of anorexia in which the sufferer imagines herself to be overweight, but rather a chronic, nervousness-induced lack of appetite. She became thin as a rail — an eighteen-year-old in a fourteen-year-old's body — and considered it a major accomplishment if she succeeded in so much as swallowing a cup of chicken broth for lunch on those Saturdays when she was condemned to be at home waiting for the next outburst or for the standard Saturday night drinking bout with its inevitable violent arguments. Her grades at college soon reflected the effects of living with this sort of time bomb — the girl who had graduated second in her high school class of six hundred seniors was now pulling mostly Cs and Bs.

Thin as a rail and her academic performance steadily deteriorating — and no one noticed!

Meanwhile, Valerie's brother Bobby had begun showing signs of relational difficulties. He completely lacked the confidence necessary to enter into even the most casual relationships with girls his age. He began drinking heavily and threatening suicide. Several times he was brought home from parties, bleeding from slashed wrists —

— and quietly put to bed.

No help was ever sought for Bobby's problem. Deny it, pretend it's "just a temporary phase" that he'll outgrow — but don't face the fact that it stems from the dysfunctional home life in which parents are so caught up in their constant game of arguing that the children are left as if exposed, unprotected, to a raging fire!

Valerie once described to me how she had pioneered the "intervention" technique some time before it had "officially" been developed. Intervention is something of a drastic measure employed to make a dysfunctional person (an alcoholic, for example) aware of the harm they are doing to themselves and those closest to them. It usually involves a team of specialists and must be planned and timed with the utmost care. Hoping against hope — and, ultimately, in vain — that someone outside the family would notice that something was very wrong, Valerie fantasized that she could persuade someone — a priest, a doctor, an older friend — to come to her house, open her parents' eyes as to what life was like for her and her brother, and ask them to mend their ways.

Unfortunately, this never happened. The mother eventually died and Valerie, with much help and encouragement from friends and spiritual mentors over the years, pulled her life together. Her brother, now in his mid-forties, has been unemployed for several years and is supported (financially) by their father. Tragically, he persists in believing what he learned as a teen: that the only guaranteed way of getting attention is to be an invalid.

Valerie's and Bobby's story is an extreme but true example of emotional neglect. Today for parents to ignore a problem such as Bobby's would be a reportable offense — "failure to provide necessary mental health services." This story points out two important things: first, the role frequently played by addiction and codependency in histories of emotional abuse and neglect.

*The presence of abuse or neglect in a family does not automatically indicate the presence of alcoholism or other substance abuse. But conversely, the presence of an alcoholic parent in a home is itself a form of abuse or, especially when the nonalcoholic parent is highly codependent, inherently constitutes neglect.*

I will go so far as to add that this applies also to the presence of a parent with a mental or emotional illness that is allowed to persist untreated.

To ignore a child's emotional needs by being

wrapped up in alcohol, an alcoholic, or a mentally or emotionally unbalanced partner is neglect.

To expect a child to live in a tense, highly charged atmosphere that militates against normal social or academic functioning and development is abuse.

The second lesson to be learned from Valerie's story is awareness of the impact of emotional abuse and neglect on teenagers as well as on young children. The song "No Son of Mine"[7] that was popular a few years ago eloquently describes the plight of a youth from an emotionally abusive home. "Soon I was living in fear every day of what might happen that night," the young man sings. This fear paralyzes. It takes over one's entire spirit, entire mind, entire nervous system. The victim's being is so galvanized toward expecting and warding off the next onslaught, the next crash of a glass shattered against the wall heralding yet another argument, that little energy or emotional space is left for normal functions.

Imagine that you are close to where a huge bomb has just been activated. It is going to unleash a powerful, noisy explosion and you have no way of protecting yourself from it. All you can do is wait while the flame slowly, inexorably burns down to where the explosion will be let loose. Moreover, you are blindfolded so that although you know that this explosion is going to occur, you do not know exactly when. Your whole body tenses while you wait.

Translate this to a mental and emotional context, and you will understand what life is like for a young person in a family with a parent who is emotionally unstable due to alcoholism or other causes. She never knows when the next explosion is going to occur. As her entire being tenses up in apprehension, bracing itself against the impact, how can she possibly spare any energy for such pursuits as an enjoyable social life? or schoolwork? or asking herself, who am I? What are my gifts and talents? What do I enjoy doing? How can I use these things to contribute to the world around me and thereby support myself? Faced with these vital questions, young people have a right to guidance and input as well as to a supportive and affirming atmosphere in which to discern their own answers. No parent can provide these things if his top priority is maintaining an unhealthy status quo relationship with a dysfunctional spouse. Both parents are caught in the web and the children are their victims.

## Captivity

When the young man in "No Son of Mine" returns home after many years, hoping for a reconciliation, he is met instead with his father's accusation, "You're no son of mine! You walked out, you left us behind!" Again this is typical in a dysfunctional, abusive family and is especially a problem that affects young people theoretically on the verge of striking out on their own. Dr. M. Scott Peck once gave a talk in which he pointed out that young people from healthy families soon leave their families to forge their own lives, whereas young people from abusive families are

likely to remain in their unpleasant homes of origin. The explanation for this seeming paradox is that
healthy families help the children to feel good about
themselves, thereby empowering them to become con-
fident, productive adults; such fortunate young people
can leave, always assured and bolstered by the love,
affirmation and support of their parents. Abusive families, in contrast, teach the children that the world is a
hostile place and convince them of their inability to
cope in it.

In this connection, psychiatrist Judith Herman
writes of "circumstances of captivity,"[8] in which pro-
longed trauma occurs. Such captivity, from which
abuse victims cannot escape, exists in prisons and
slave camps, as well as in brothels and some religious cults. It can also exist in families and especially
victimizes children, who obviously cannot escape, as
well as older teenagers whose parents have emotionally crippled them so that they are unable to survive
in any other environment: they have "normalized the
abnormal."

The dynamic operating in such an abusive family
is one of control. It is *centripetal*, seeking always to
draw its members inward and retain them there, in
the same way that a fly-killing apparatus attracts the
unsuspecting insects and paralyzes them. The normal
family is *centrifugal*, operating with a dynamic of *freedom*, empowering its members toward independence
and self-sufficiency.

Abusive parents have several weapons in their arsenal with which to retain control over their chil-

dren. One incapacitating weapon is the unpredictability of the traumas they cause. Clarissa Pinkola Estes,[9] discussing the loss of the self-protective instinct, describes an experiment conducted in the 1960s that was intended to shed light on the human "flight instinct." The scientists wired half the bottom of a cage so that the dog in the cage would receive a shock whenever it set foot on that side of the cage. As a result of the shocks, the dog learned to stay on the other, "shock-free" side of the cage. Then the scientists reversed the wiring. Again, the dog quickly learned to stay on the other side. Next the scientists wired the cage floor so that the dog would receive random shocks. At first the dog was confused; then it panicked; at last it simply gave up trying to avoid the shocks. Finally, however, the scientists opened the cage door. Contrary to what they expected, the dog did not rush to escape but instead continued to lie there being randomly shocked. The scientists thus concluded that a creature exposed to violence will adapt to it, so that even when the violence stops or the creature is given the chance to escape, it will not do so. The healthy instinct to flee is diminished.

With human beings things differ little if at all. Abused children (like women victims of domestic violence) learn to adapt to violence, to consider it normal, to expect it sooner or later; they are sapped of the will and energy to escape.

My friend Valerie never knew when the next major disaster would occur. Would a sarcastic, stony silence be reigning when she arrived home because her father had returned from work five minutes later than he had expected to? Would an argument be raging at the dinner table, precipitated by her mother's feeding a dangerous chicken bone to Bobby's beloved pet dog?

Another favorite control weapon is threats. The abuser may threaten to hurt the victim, the victim's property, pet, and so forth. My mother, an expert in the use of this weapon as described in my "Pig Pen" story above, employed an additional variation on it. A manipulatively suicidal person, she controlled the family by threatening to kill herself, on occasion ostentatiously writing a "suicide note." Her every whim and demand was acceded to because that ultimate threat always loomed. Another form of threat, which began making its appearance when I was in my late teens and thus in a position to think about leaving home, was more direct: If I ever — even after I graduated from college and got a job — left home for any reason other than to get married, I would be disowned. This threat had repercussions that I will save for a later chapter.

## Notes

1. *About Emotional Abuse and Neglect of Children,* A Scriptographic Booklet (S. Deerfield, MA: Channing L. Bete, Inc., 1991), p. 11.

2. *Interdisciplinary Glossary of Child Abuse,* quoted in James Garbarino and Anne C. Garbarino, *Emotional Maltreatment of Children,* 2d ed. (Chicago: National Committee to Prevent Child Abuse), p. 18.

3. Garbarino and Garbarino, *Emotional Maltreatment of Children*, p. 19.

4. A complete chart of "Who Reports" is given in Diane D. Broadhurst, *Educators, Schools, and Child Abuse* (Chicago: National Committee to Prevent Child Abuse, 1986, 1991), pp. 26–27.

5. Patricia M. Crittenden, *Preventing Child Neglect* (Chicago: National Committee to Prevent Child Abuse, 1992), p. 3.

6. Ibid., p. 2.

7. "No Son of Mine," copyright 1991 by Anthony Banks Ltd., Philip Collins Ltd., Michael Rutherford Ltd.

8. Judith Lewis Herman, M.D., *Trauma and Recovery* (New York: Basic Books, 1992), p. 74.

9. Clarissa Pinkola Estes, *Women Who Run with the Wolves* (New York: Ballantine Books, 1992), pp. 244–45.

# 2

# No One Deserves Abuse

Whether your experiences of abuse have been similar to or different from mine, all of us who have been abused as children have this in common: We did not deserve to be abused.

Children deserve and require *discipline*. "Discipline" should not be equated with the mindless sort of punishment that is really nothing more than revenge. Children need encouragement; they need love, caring example and respect.

In 1993 the American Catholic bishops issued a Pastoral Message to Families entitled *Follow the Way of Love*. In it they say:

- *Parents:* not only do your children need discipline and love, they need the example of adults whose behavior demonstrates their caring. Put your children first in making decisions about family life.

- *Children and youth:* you have the right to expect love, guidance, discipline, and respect from your parents and elders.[1]

## Abuse and Discipline: The Thin Line between Them

Every parent has a right to discipline his or her child, and every child has a right to be disciplined properly.

But no parent has the right to abuse, demean, or humiliate a child.

Discipline is important:

- It encourages appropriate behavior.

- It helps to prevent problems that could arise as the child grows older.

- It instills a lifelong sense of self-discipline.

- It forms the child into the adult of the future.

Discipline helps children develop self-control and orderliness; it teaches them to respect the rights of others; it helps them to build their self-esteem and become self-reliant and to express emotions appropriately.

Discipline promotes *competence,* which, as we saw in chapter 1, is the quality that empowers an individual to function harmoniously and productively in society.

Abuse, on the other hand, does not promote competence — instead it undermines the development of competence by establishing fear and poor self-esteem as the bases for the individual's relationship with the world.

Discipline takes the long-term view: How will this

intervention help my child eventually to take his or her place in society as a harmonious and productive adult?

Abuse takes the short-term view: My immediate convenience is at stake; how can I best achieve it?

Discipline *and* abuse are both taught by example.

## Honor Thy Children...

Pope John Paul II in his *Letter to Families* commemorating the Year of the Family (1994) writes of the *honor* due to children from their parents:

> ... Indirectly we can speak of the honor owed to children by their parents. "To honor" means to acknowledge! ... Honor is essentially an attitude of unselfishness.... If the Fourth Commandment demands that honor should be shown to our father and mother, it also makes this demand out of concern for the good of the family. Precisely for this reason, however, it makes demands of the parents themselves. You parents, the divine precept seems to say, should act in such a way that your life will merit the honor (and the love) of your children! ... Ultimately then we are speaking of mutual honor. The commandment "honor your father and mother" indirectly tells parents: Honor your sons and your daughters. They deserve this because they are alive, because they are who they are.... [2]

On Sundays we often pray for an increase in respect for life in all its stages. We must remember that this includes respect for children, from the newborn right up to the young adult about to leave the parental home. The American bishops remind us:

> Children in the family share equal dignity as persons with the adults. They too are part of the covenant of mutuality. Parents can demonstrate this by treating children with respect, giving them responsibilities, listening seriously to their thoughts and feelings.[3]

Abuse deprives the child of his or her personhood. It dichotomizes the family into two distinct groups: *adults,* who have the *right* to *receive* respect, honor and obedience from their children and at the same time to treat them any way they please; and *children,* who have the *obligation* to *give* their parents unconditional and unquestioning respect, honor and obedience.

Such an approach to family functioning negates the possibility of disciplining through good example and exposes the child to the chronic hypocrisy of the "Do as I say, not as I do" philosophy.

### Good Example as Discipline

I mentioned earlier that discipline is taught by example. Good example is the most effective way to instill good habits: for example, good manners, tidiness or punctuality. The "Do as I say ... " philosophy, on the other hand, draws an invisible but indelible line that stands to keep the child forever a child. "This behavior is for children; that behavior is for adults." Several possible unfortunate consequences can issue from this attitude:

(1) The child never internalizes the correct reasons for good behavior and thus adopts the behavior out of fear of external punishment rather than out of an internalized system of values or self-discipline.

(2) The child never learns when she crosses the line from child to adult, since this approach to child-rearing does not have as its goal preparing her for mature adulthood.

(3) The child does cross the line to "adulthood" and now assumes allegedly "adult" behavior: the bad manners and other undesirable behavior — including, eventually, the abuse of his own spouse and children — learned from the parents' example.

A child who does not witness the giving of respect through being a recipient of respect will never learn how to give respect. She will learn to give servile obedience, perhaps, but not the authentic respect born of belief in the inherent dignity of the other person. The child who is *ordered around* (while, of course, being told to say "Please" and "Thank you" to adults!) instead of *asked* to do something becomes nothing more than an obedient automaton.

## Obedience and "Poisonous Pedagogy"

Renowned author on child abuse Alice Miller writes of the "poisonous pedagogy" that deifies absolute obedience to parents and that insists on the parents' right to complete control over and unconditional respect from their children.[4] John Bradshaw refers to the "insidiousness of total obedience" and reminds us of its consequences, which range from the "doormat"-like individual to such phenomena as Nazism and Jonestown.[5] Tragically, poisonous pedagogy instills in the child distorted principles that the child carries over into his belief system in adulthood.

Until I graduated from high school we lived in an apartment building in which the mail boxes were on the ground floor. Every day my mother would order me, "Nancy, go down and get the mail!" And every day I obeyed immediately.

When it came time for me to choose a college, I wanted very much to study liturgical music, Latin and theology. In order to pursue these studies I would have had to live away at college — no institution offering these courses was located within commuting distance of our house. When I mentioned my plans to my mother, she responded, "You can't do that. You're not going to live away at college."

Of course, I dropped my plans without question; after all, that was how I had been programmed! Accordingly, the gifted liturgical musician, the high school "Latin scholar" who took the Latin medal at graduation and won first or second prize in every Latin contest she entered during her four years of high school, allowed herself to be manipulated into attending a "safe," urban women's college that offered neither Latin nor music!

At the age of twenty-two I reached a crisis when it struck me that I had internalized no positive values. My only motivation for doing the "right" thing was fear of punishment if I disobeyed orders. I was now too old to be spanked. On what were my decisions to be based?

### Long- and Short-Term Thinking

Earlier I identified discipline with the long-term view and abuse with the short-term view of childrearing. Child psychiatrist Dr. Gary May points out:

> *Discipline is designed to help the child control and change his behavior, thereby guiding the child into adulthood.* Abuse, on the other hand, does not take the child's future needs into consideration. It is not designed to help the child learn socially acceptable ways of expressing natural desires and drives. Abuse dumps an adult's feelings on the child in a harmful or neglectful way. This satisfies the adult's needs, but it does not satisfy the child's needs.[6]

Typically, the *high-functioning family* thinks in *long-range* terms and sets long-term goals. Secure and high-functioning parents regard obedience not as an end in itself, but as a means to an end. They establish consistent norms that promote such goods as safety, consideration, or the mutual comfort and convenience of all who live under one roof, and set forth for the child these goods as the reason for following the norms.

The *dysfunctional family,* in contrast, uses *short-term* thinking. Dysfunctional, abusive parents beat or frighten their children into perfect "obedience" for their own convenience or to impress the world with their "well-behaved" children. They do not consider the long-range formation of the child's personality. My friend Valerie's parents sacrificed the long-range goal of mental and emotional health for their children in favor of the short-term goal of preserving the family's reputation; this concern for "appearances" is often a prominent consideration in the dynamic of denial. Short-term thinking is itself bad example. It is also a common consequence of the abusive treatment we have received, particularly if we lived in addictive homes, that we lack the ability to think in the long term, to formulate long-term plans and set long-term goals. After all, we have conditioned ourselves only to try to survive from one emotional onslaught to the next.

In Matthew's Gospel (Matthew 25:14–30) Jesus tells the parable of the talents, in which those to whom the talents had been entrusted are judged and rewarded according to how well they had used them. The main "talent" with which God provides parents, the chief aspect of their lives in which God will be interested, is their children. The parent who, like the worthless, lazy slave in Jesus' story, buries the talent is the parent who is afraid or unwilling to let the child go: the insecure, unadventurous, unimaginative parent who buries the child's personality under his or her own short-term needs for convenient obedience instead of taking the risk and helping the child to flourish.

### Respect and Self-Esteem

"You only get as much respect as you demand." My eighth-grade teacher, Sister Rosaline, was fond of saying this to us girls by way of advising us how to conduct ourselves with boys. By "demand" she meant not a stern admonition but an attitude — an awareness that one deserves to be treated with dignity and respect — that by its very nature sets boundaries for behavior.

Just as a child who is never given responsibilities in the home does not become able and willing to assume life's responsibilities the minute he reaches the magic age of twenty-one, so too an unloved, unrespected child does not suddenly regard herself as worthy of respect when she becomes an adult. She develops no sense of boundaries, no sense of limits to the disrespectful and denigrating treatment she "deserves" or is obliged to tolerate.

Take the child who is threatened with drastic physical punishment. Even if the punishment never materializes, the mere fact that an adult in authority considered this treatment appropriate may cause the child to grow up believing that her body is "fair game" for anything. My mother often threatened to "bend my fingers back" for minor transgressions, and it was not until I saw our Bishop John McGann cringe when I mentioned this during the taping of a TV program on child abuse that it was confirmed for me that this was an unacceptable method of punishment.

I am firmly convinced that sexual promiscuity results not so much from lax upbringing as from the abusive parenting that (a) leaves a girl with no sense of self-respect about her body (b) causes her to look outside the parental home for the love she does not receive there. Ironically, what saved me from becoming promiscuous was the belief, droned into me from an early age, that I was "an ugly child" and therefore quite undesirable to the opposite sex!

## Abuse and Religion

To treat children in such a way that we disregard our responsibility to respect and honor them is to treat them as *possessions* rather than as *people*.

The Rev. Dr. Marie Fortune points out that children are not something we own — they are part of our community of God. When we baptize children we do not merely "give them a name," "wash away original sin from their soul" or fulfill a family custom; rather, we initiate them into our community of faith and affirm their dignity as members of the people of God.

Sadly, child abuse is sometimes perpetrated in the name of religion. Any of the forms of emotional abuse described in chapter 1 can be couched in a religious context.

For example, religion can be invoked in ridicule, rejection or other blows to self-esteem. I received First Communion at the age of seven and, for a long time thereafter, went to daily Mass and Communion. One day my mother, with that look of hatred to which by then I had become accustomed, challenged me as to why I received Communion every day. The implication was clear: You had to be "good" in order to go to Communion, and I was far from the mark.

Here was a seven-year-old, who had already been so beaten down that she was scared stiff of committing the slightest infraction, being told that she did not deserve to receive Jesus in the Eucharist. Strangely enough, however, I persisted in doing so; my father accompanied me to these daily Masses, and his implied acceptance of my practice affirmed for me that it was all right.

Religion is a prime context for expression of the "Do as I say, not as I do" hypocrisy mentioned above. An abusive parent adds insult to injury by lecturing a child about obligation toward religious practice while continuing the abusive behavior. My friend Valerie, a religious person all during her high school and early years of college, reached a crisis when her faith system provided no answers, no support for her in coping with a home thrown into chaos by her mother's addiction and emotional problems. Her "re-

ligious comfort zone" had been one in which God
rewards those who keep the commandments, practice
their devotions regularly and so forth; now suddenly
she found herself tossed out of it like a pile of pins
emptied from a cup and scattered on a counter top.
Valerie stopped attending Mass regularly, and her parents began to nag and criticize her for this. Here
was a "home" in which the chief gods were alcohol and codependency, with the parents insisting on
the children's formal observance of religion while they
themselves totally disregarded their obligation to help
their children develop into the "human being fully
alive" that St. Irenaeus said is the glory of God.

As the Rev. Dr. Marie Fortune has stated, abuse
wrapped in religiosity is blasphemous.

Perhaps the most common manifestation of emotional abuse in religious terms involves "terrorizing" — frightening children with the notion of God as
an avenging judge who notes down the tiniest trans-
gression in a big book, has a very long memory, and
withdraws his love if you disobey him.

I do not advocate the "warm fuzzy" religion cur-
rently popular, the kind that revels in the "Jesus loves
me" philosophy, consists of a vague injunction to "feel
good" about everyone, and ignores the uncomfortable
fact that our relationship with God gives us certain
obligations as well as rights, and indeed inevitably
entails the cross. But I do believe strongly that an individual's conception of God forms the basis of that
person's relationship with the world, and that therefore it is vitally important for parents to recognize

their responsibility and their primary role in forming a child's picture of God. This picture is shaped not only by what a parent actually teaches a child about God, but, more importantly, by the kind of treatment the parent gives the child. As John Bradshaw writes, the child depends on its parents for survival. For the sake of self-preservation the child *must* believe that the parents are omnipotent. "The magical part of the child's thinking *deifies the parents*. They are gods, all-powerful, almighty and all-protecting."[7]

Thus, the way a parent treats her child will inevitably be the way that child sees God: to the very young child, still at the stage of forming primary impressions of the world around him and totally dependent on that big creature called the parent, the parent *is* God. The child who experiences love and affirmation from his parents will envision God as a loving, supportive parent. The child whose parents abuse and punish her will form a picture of God as a judgmental, avenging authority figure.

The American Catholic bishops tell parents:

You carry out the mission of the church of the home in ordinary ways when: . . .

- You *love* and never give up believing in the value of another person. Before young ones hear the Word of God preached from the pulpit, they form a picture of God drawn from their earliest experiences of being loved by parents, grandparents, godparents, and other family members.[8]

Just as children learn discipline more from observed practice than from preaching, so in the same way do they first learn the word of God. The parent who only loves her child *conditionally* — who loves *only if* the child behaves, does well in school, practices the piano and so forth, and who withdraws her love when these conditions are not met — tarnishes the true picture of a God who loves us *unconditionally* and forgives us time and time again. It goes without saying that the parent who shows no love for her child under any conditions presents the child with a toxic image of God.

Jesus said, "If any of you put a stumbling block before one of these little ones who believe in me, it would be better for you if a great millstone were fastened around your neck and you were drowned in the depths of the sea" (Matthew 18:6). So strongly did Jesus judge those who lead children astray through abuse perpetrated in the name of religion. Powerful food for thought, indeed.

## Notes

1. *Follow the Way of Love*, A Pastoral Message of the U.S. Catholic Bishops to Families on the Occasion of the United Nations 1994 International Year of the Family (Washington, D.C.: United States Catholic Conference, 1994), p. 27.

2. Pope John Paul II, *Letter to Families* (Washington, D.C.: United States Catholic Conference, 1994), p. 17.

3. *Follow the Way of Love*, p. 21.

4. Alice Miller, *For Your Own Good: Hidden Cruelty in Child-Rearing and the Roots of Violence,* 3d ed. (New York: The Noonday Press, 1990), p. 59.

5. John Bradshaw, *Bradshaw On: The Family* (Deerfield Beach, FL: Health Communications, Inc., 1988), p. 19.

6. Gary May, *Child Discipline: Guidelines for Parents* (Chicago: National Committee to Prevent Child Abuse, 1979), p. 7.

7. Bradshaw, *Bradshaw On: The Family,* p. 9.

8. *Follow the Way of Love,* p. 9.

# 3

# The Legacy of Abuse

By the time I entered my teens, I concluded that my mother must have been right: hours of sitting on the sidelines at dances watching my friends have all the fun drove in the painful confirmation that the ugly child had become an ugly teenager. No one wanted to dance with "Monkeyface."

Many years and very few dates later I met a man who turned my life around. Peter did not find me aesthetically challenged: he found me "unusual." Since he came from a country where the variety of facial types is limited, I interpreted this as a positive judgment. Life took on a whole new meaning for me: at last I had found love and joined the "normal" human race.

I moved in together with Peter — which meant relocating from England, where I had been living for some years, to Sweden. We would get married some day, he said, but not immediately. Far from being disappointed, I was elated that he would consider marrying me at all. Old self-concepts die hard, and I actually accepted myself as an intrinsically inferior person who had no right to expect anyone to make the public, life-long commitment to me that marriage entails — even if, on another level, I saw myself as no longer "ugly" and realized I *could* attract a man.

It speaks tellingly of the new, refreshing level of self-confidence I had attained that when Mike, an American acquaintance of Peter from London, commented about me, "Where do you find these gorgeous women?" I initially took this at face value, as a compliment.

Then the penny of suspicion dropped inside my head.

"You don't suppose Mike was being sarcastic?" I asked Peter.

"Oh, he was!"

I should have known. My blossoming self-confidence suddenly plummeted like the temperature on a January day before an approaching storm. So, I had been fooling myself all along; I really *was* unattractive after all. Mike's "compliment" wasn't the last. Peter moved in circles that held superficial attractiveness in high regard, and several variations on this denigrating theme were faithfully repeated to me as they were offered. Fortunately, Peter liked me anyway.

Peter, however, was very involved in his business. "Business comes first" — that motto should have been engraved in gold above our door. This entailed, for example, that he could not acknowledge my existence to some of his female potential business associates: after all, he had to charm them into becoming involved in his business projects, and his charm would have lost much of its force if these women had thought he was unavailable. It meant that when our son Anton was born he came to fetch us from the hospital long after the other women discharged that day had gone home — the phone kept ringing and the calls might have been important for business. It also meant a major guilt trip for me if I expressed my needs for attention and companionship — how incredibly selfish of me when business demanded so much attention!

## Vicious Cycle I: From Abused Child to Abused Adult

And so I spent those years with Peter as I spent my childhood — living in an emotional vacuum. It's a sad but real fact: Abuse is a cyclical phenomenon. The abused child becomes an abused adult.

Jack Walters, a Jesuit priest and psychotherapist, describes how, as children, we learned certain "laws" or principles that enabled us to survive and relate within our families of origin. As we grow up, we take these principles, which were valid for a specific situation, and apply them to the world at large. The child from a supportive, affirming family will grow into the adult world with positive expectations. The child from an abusive family will take negative expectations into the adult world: all relationships will be "based on nastiness, violence and victimization."[1] As the abused child enters adulthood, she stands the risk of continuing to play the chief role she learned in her family of origin: that of the abuse victim.

As a child Pam was physically punished whenever she did anything wrong.[2] The beating was followed by forgiveness — Pam "earned" her forgiveness by being abused. She felt better and cleaner after these punishments than at any other time.

When she grew up and got married, Pam wanted to re-create that good, clean post-punishment feeling. Therefore she made sure that each evening when her husband came home, she had a long list of wrong behaviors to recite to him. After she recited her sins to her husband, he punished and forgave her.

When we expect the worst from other people, we attract it. We are drawn to people who treat us the way we are accustomed to being treated: if we are accustomed to being abused, we are suspicious of, and reject, anyone who tries to treat us with the respect we deserve.

In chapter 2 I stated that a child who lives without respect or love does not suddenly perceive herself as deserving of respect and love the minute she reaches the magical age of adulthood. Such a child has internalized the negative message inculcated in her by her parents: to exist without love but with abuse is her lot in life.

## Poor Self-Esteem and Low Expectations of Life

My good friend Msgr. Jim Lisante tells the story of an engaged couple that he was preparing for marriage.[3] After the couple had met with him a few times for marriage preparation, he began to suspect that something was not quite right, and so he contrived to see the young woman alone on one occasion. Sure enough, it turned out that her fiance was abusing her both physically and verbally.

When this came to light, Msgr. Jim told the bride-to-be that he couldn't in good conscience officiate at a wedding under such circumstances.

"Oh, but Father Jim, we have to get married!" she said.

When he asked her why, she replied, "Because he's the best thing I'm going to find!"

This young woman had grown up with such low expectations from life, and had been allowed to develop such poor self-esteem, that she honestly believed that she deserved nothing better than a husband who abused her. Having not experienced warmth and affection in her family of origin, she now sought it in marriage — at any price.

I winced with pain when I first heard this story, because that young woman could so easily have been me. I felt that I "had" to get married because it was the only way (as I mentioned at the end of chapter 1) I could leave our unpleasant home without being disowned. What would have been so dreadful about that? When your self-confidence has received a daily battering, you end up doubting your ability even to support yourself financially — therefore you don't dare risk losing that "safety net," however horrible it may be in other ways. All these factors then converge to ingrain in you a "beggars-can't-be-choosers" mentality.

Before I met Peter, I dated a man named Paul. This relationship was characterized chiefly by two things:

(1) If I ever did anything to displease Paul (for example, pulling up something other than a weed in his garden; overcooking a meal; not eating enough of the food he prepared) he reacted with extreme anger — never physically hurting me, but abusing me verbally and/or withdrawing into a shell, looking like a seething cauldron about to explode. I spent much of the time cringing, wondering what I would manage to do wrong next.

(2) We never met any of Paul's friends or family. If we happened to meet in public where there were other people around that he knew, he ignored me. This was a taken-for-granted procedure: my looks weren't up to his accustomed standard.

Looking back on this and on similar situations in my life, I find it striking that I never saw escape as an option — it never occurred to me that I could simply walk out. The person who has lived with abuse from Day One assumes that this sort of relationship is "normal" for her and that she will never find, nor does she deserve, anything better.

## Shame: A Constant Companion

John Bradshaw draws an important distinction between *guilt* and *shame*.

> Guilt says I've *done* something wrong; shame says there *is* something wrong with me. Guilt says I've *made* a mistake; shame says I *am* a mistake. Guilt says what I *did* was not good; shame says I *am* no good.[4]

Guilt, in other words, separates my *actions* from my *self*. If I have done something wrong and have healthy *guilt*, that means that I am able to acknowledge that *what I have done* was wrong. Healthy guilt is an emotion that "results from behaving in a manner contrary to our beliefs and values";[5] as such, it is intimately bound up with our conscience.

Toxic *shame*, on the other hand, makes my wrong action coextensive with my entire being; it says that *I* am bad. *Healthy shame* — which, as defined by Bradshaw, is really akin to humility — helps me to acknowledge that I am imperfect and to accept myself as such — after all, no one is perfect! *Toxic shame* makes a (real or imagined) imperfection into my existential identity. "To have shame as an identity is to believe that one's being is flawed, that one is defective as a human being."[6] From this kind of shame there is neither escape nor forgiveness.

Toxic shame is a legacy of abusive parenting. The child whose parents drastically overreact to the child's slightest behavioral imperfections develops massive shame feelings that plague him throughout his life.

You will recall my story in chapter 1 about being threatened with exile to the "Pig Pen." A different but equally terrifying episode of overreaction occurred when I was perhaps three or four years old. My mother and I were in a playground near our apartment building and I stood alone while my mother carried on a conversation with a neighbor. All of a sudden I uttered the word "stupid." I don't know why: I wasn't calling any particular person stupid, I simply came out with the word. Some time prior to this my mother had issued dire warnings about saying "stupid" — apparently it was one of the worst words you could utter, and its use would merit unspeakable punishments. So, perhaps I said "stupid" simply in order to get attention; I may have thought that the conversation had gone on too long.

The unspeakable punishment was swift in coming. My mother whirled round, grabbed me by the arm and, in a great fury, dragged me upstairs to our apartment. She then took a bottle of "thumb stuff" — I never did know the correct name of it, but it was a burning liquid of which you painted a bit on a child's thumb to discourage the sucking habit — held my head back and mouth open and poured all the liquid down my throat.

What made the deepest impression on me was not the physical discomfort from the burning liquid but the terrifying spectacle of this raging person before whom I was totally helpless and who held me in her power — literally in a vicelike grip. Looking back on this incident and reflecting on others, I realize now that I was at the "mercy" of a sadistic individual.

Experiences such as these carried severe repercussions well into my adult life, most painfully affecting my attitude toward and performance at work in various positions in which I was employed. If a boss ever questioned my work or pointed out the slightest imperfection, I froze, panicked and assumed I was about to be fired. Each day I would arrive at work with my stomach in a knot, worried about whether I would find a note on my desk questioning something I did. Gradually I would doubt my competence to do the work at all (even though I actually was highly qualified). My usual reaction was to act obsequious and apologetic. I never interpreted a question simply *as* a question without assuming that it implied a major personal criticism; nor did it ever occur to me either to challenge a boss's criticism or to negotiate, that is, to ask and learn how I could improve something. After all, I had concluded, such people can't be negotiated with — what they say goes, even when their criticism seems unjust or exaggerated, and I am powerless to influence the situation, even if I end up losing my job for a minor imperfection.

Did I really ever work for such ogres? Of course not — but this is the pattern of thinking that gets ingrained in someone who as a helpless child has had to bear the uncontrolled rage of a parent who punishes in the same way that some overzealous soul might use a sledgehammer to kill a mosquito. This is the toxic shame that is the legacy of emotional abuse.

## A Self-Fulfilling Prophecy

"You're stupid!"

"You're an ugly child!"

"You'll never amount to anything!"

Abusive epithets hurled at a child in anger can turn out to be self-fulfilling prophecies as the child to whom they are addressed internalizes them and unconsciously lives up to these negative expectations.

A colleague at one of my jobs was a lovely woman named Joan. As a child, Joan did not do particularly well in school. The problem turned out to be poor eyesight — she simply couldn't see to read well, particularly the school blackboard — but no one ever bothered to check this out. Instead, Joan's mother continually called her stupid, and would even grab her hair and pound her head on the table, yelling, "You're stupid! You're stupid!" By the time the real cause of the problem was discovered, it was too late. Joan persisted in thinking of herself as stupid and never reached her full potential in her work life.

The girl called "ugly" compounds the problem by not taking sufficient care of her appearance — what's the point when any effort would be a drop in the bucket anyway? — and can even end up developing an "ugly," uncharming personality. I speak from experience. If a film had been made of my life in my teens or early twenties, it could have been titled *I Was a Teenage Drip*. When not acting obsequious or trying to hide or apologize for the mere fact of my existence, I was abrupt and abrasive, chemically pure of any social skills whatsoever. Only my few close friends ever saw the witty and sociable person that lay hidden underneath all this.

A recent, telling incident illustrates the close relationship between inner self-image and external appearance. A group of us who have been friends for decades were sitting around looking at photo albums going back many years — pictures taken at our various gatherings that served as periodic reunions when we lived far apart from one another. Indicating some photos of myself taken when I was in my twenties, I commented that I seemed to take after my paternal aunts, all of whom got better looking as they got older, since I certainly looked better now than I had when those pictures were taken. "Or maybe," countered my friend Joe, "you have a higher opinion of yourself now than you did then."

Whether Joe meant that my improved self-image made me more accepting of the way I look now, or that my improved self-image actually manifested itself in an improved physical appearance, the message is the same: inner healing had taken place that affected my "only-skin-deep" level as well — the spell of the self-fulfilling prophecy had been broken.

## Vicious Cycle II:
## From Abused Child to Abusive Adult

Children who see others being abused, or who have been abused themselves, are six times more likely to abuse a spouse or child when they become adults than those raised in a home without violence.[7]

Alice Miller asserts that not *most* but *all* people who abuse their children have experienced similar traumas in their own childhood.[8] This is one of the saddest and most destructive legacies of child abuse: The abused child becomes an abusive parent or abusive spouse, thereby continuing the cycle of abuse into the next generation.

Two main factors are at work in this perpetuation dynamic:

(1) *"Because abusive parenting is all [abusive parents] have known, they repeat it with their own children."*[9] Our parents are our primary educators in parenting. The way we were parented will usually be the way we parent our own children. People learn to regard the abuse they experienced in childhood as "for their own good"[10] — it was not maltreatment but deserved punishment. Alice Miller describes the inner dynamic typical of such a parent:

"It is my duty to discipline my child, and I do this in exactly or much the same way as my mother did to me. And after all, I've turned out all right, haven't I? I graduated with good marks, I've become involved in church work and the peace movement, and I've always spoken out against injustice. Only in the case of my own children I couldn't avoid having to beat them, though I didn't really want to.... I hope I haven't harmed them, just as it didn't do me any harm."[11]

I can well identify with the "for your own good" mindset. Until I was well into my teens, having so often been commended for being so "well behaved," I credited my parents with my wonderful, strict upbringing — they disciplined me to make sure I always toed the line. It took a while before it dawned on me that this "exemplary upbringing" consisted of the instilling of fear to prevent me claiming my own identity as an autonomous human being with all the rights that this entails.

(2) *As abused children, the parents repressed the true meaning of what was being done to them.* This was a necessary survival mechanism: the young child could not have coped with the full force of the significance of the maltreatment he was experiencing. Instead he had to repress it and accept the abusive treatment. Could the child have shown anger over the abuse? No: for this to happen "the child needs the confidence based on experience that he will not be killed as a result."[12]

In order for healing to take place in our lives, and in order to avoid our perpetuation of the vicious cycle of abuse to the next generation, it is imperative that we face the facts and name what has been done to us. This process plays an important role in the whole dynamic of *forgiveness,* as we will see in the next chapter.

## Notes

1. Jack Walters, *Jesus Healer of Our Inner World* (New York: Crossroad Publishing Co., 1995), pp. 139–40.

2. Pam's story is taken from Christine Comstock Herbruck, *Breaking the Cycle of Child Abuse* (Minneapolis: Winston Press, 1979), pp. 47–48.

3. Fr. James P. Lisante, *Of Life and Love,* 2d ed. (Mineola: Resurrection Press, 1991), p. 51.

4. Bradshaw, *Bradshaw On: The Family,* p. 2.

5. John Bradshaw, *Healing the Shame that Binds You* (Deerfield Beach, FL: Health Communications, Inc., 1988), p. 17.

6. Ibid., p. vii.

7. J. Kaufman and E. Ziegler, "The intergenerational transmission of child abuse," New York, 1989.

8. Alice Miller, *Banished Knowledge: Facing Childhood Injuries* (New York: Anchor Books/Doubleday, 1990), p. 190.

9. Anne Cohn Donnelly, D.P.H., *It Shouldn't Hurt to Be a Child,* rev. ed. (Chicago: National Committee to Prevent Child Abuse, 1987), p. 6.

10. Miller, *Banished Knowledge,* p. 8.

11. Ibid., pp. 195–96.

12. Ibid., p. 194.

# 4

# Healing:
# The Journey
# Worth the Risk

Alice Miller has changed her mind. Originally, she believed that it was not possible for the vicious cycle of child abuse to be broken. Now she is convinced that

> infectious diseases need not spread if the virus is known. Injuries can heal and need not be passed on, provided they are not ignored. It is perfectly possible to awaken from sleep and . . . to be open to the messages from our children that can help us never again to destroy life but rather to protect it and allow it to blossom.[1]

Here, then, is the good news: It *is* possible both to heal the psychological and spiritual wounds inflicted by the emotional abuse we experienced as children and to break the vicious cycle of maltreatment so that we do not carry over the abusive behavior to our own children. We will always have scars, yes, but those scars will be our badges of glory from the battle, and we will rid ourselves of the debilitating wounds that vitiate our daily lives and especially our relationships, whether with those close to us as family or friends or with our colleagues in the workplace.

Note that Dr. Miller says that injuries can be healed and prevented from spreading *provided they are not ignored.* One of the most insidious factors to militate against our seeking healing for psychological wounds is the dynamic of *denial* — the refusal to accept the fact that the problem exists. Denial can be promoted by the wish to "save face," by an unwillingness to admit that our parents were not perfect, or by resistance to the hard work that the healing process will necessarily entail. Whatever its cause, the effect is always the same: the problem persists, both in our own lives and down to the next generation.

Whenever I give talks on abuse and addiction to engaged couples I stress one thing above all: they must always be honest with themselves. The shame is not in *having* a problem, but in being too proud, too lazy or too whatever to *admit* that one has a problem and to get help for it.

The National Committee to Prevent Child Abuse urges victims of child abuse to "seek help — no matter how long ago the abuse occurred,"[2] and even the American Catholic bishops assure us:

There is no shame in seeking help for family problems, whether it be in the form of counseling, educational programs, or support groups.[3]

# Seek a Supportive, Healing Relationship

They say that a gifted sculptor can look at a block of marble and visualize the work of art within it; the sculptor's task is simply to free the figure from the massive, nondescript block.

This is the liberating experience that awaits a person severely damaged in spirit by abuse. If you are such a person, I urge you to find your own gifted sculptor who will help to free your inner beauty from the massive block of hurt, shame and disappointment that abuse has built up around you. This can be a friend, pastoral minister, confessor, spiritual director, or professional counselor or therapist.

The person who guides and accompanies you on this journey of healing must be:

- *someone you can trust* — someone who will respect the confidentiality of the information you will be sharing.

- *someone who makes you feel "safe"* — someone who will be accepting of the pain you experienced in the past and of the wounds it has left in your present life.

- *someone you can see on a fairly regular basis.*

- *someone who can help you make connections* — someone who will provide insight into how your present ways of thinking and relating are distortions based on the wrong "laws" and principles that you internalized in order to enable you to survive in a dysfunctional environment. This person will help you to see the lies you absorbed about yourself — "I'm stupid," "I'm ugly," "I will be thrown away/fired/annihilated/totally rejected if I . . . " — for the falsehoods they are.

- *someone who is honest and who will help you to be honest.*

It has been said that "the longest journey of all is the journey inward." The process of looking within to discover the roots of our wounds is one of facing the cross. It means that we come to understand where Jesus was in our lives while we were suffering. This is painful and we must risk the pain. We like to appear "in control," "on top of things," and not admit that people have hurt us — but we must let go of this if we are seriously to embark on our journey of healing. I strongly recommend against "feel-good" therapy, in which the person guiding you mainly lets you vent your anger and leaves you focused on the unfairness of the abusive treatment you received without taking it any further.

My "sculptor" was a curate at the parish in eastern England in which I had become active. I first was moved to confide in Anthony about my past at around the same time that Peter became involved with the woman he would eventually marry. Even though Anthony and I already had a good relationship that included confession and spiritual direction, I did not at first find it easy to open up to him about this other aspect of my life. After all, I was the witty person who always managed to share a few insightful and amusing tidbits at the parish renewal weekends; I was an excellent lector; I played an important role in the parish-level listening sessions to prepare for the Synod on the Laity. How could I suddenly reveal that I had been a "weakling" (for so I thought of myself) at the mercy of an abusive parent? But in this new role Anthony turned out to be a soul-friend blessed with Christ's own gift for recognizing the potential in the most unlikely places and for nourishing and cultivating it. Gradually I revealed the feelings of inferiority and unworthiness, the absurd guilt at having let so many people down by being born aesthetically challenged. The deep prayer he taught me brought the release that came from being able to mourn for myself, to admit other people's power to hurt me, and to realize that Jesus had been suffering with me the whole time.

Shortly after I returned to America, I met another priest who was to become my good friend, Msgr. Jim Lisante. As with Anthony, I first knew Jim through my parish and then through my work in publishing. Eventually he offered me a job working for him in a diocesan agency. My relationship with him has been one of amazing healing in the area of workplace situations. He has given me space to be myself, to make the job "my own" and in so doing occasionally to make mistakes. I no longer live in fear of being terminated by a boss for the slightest imperfection.

## Breaking the Vicious Cycle

When I was in my early twenties I determined that if I ever had a child, I would prove that I could be a better mother than the one I had. This was easier said than done. Our parents, unavoidably, are our primary educators in parenting. Despite our conscious efforts to parent our children differently from the way we were parented, there are times when a child's behavior elicits an instant reaction from us. Those are times when we don't, indeed can't, stop and analyze how we should react; rather, we respond instantaneously and unconsciously — in the same way our parents responded to us in a similar situation.

I say this not to discourage you from attempting to break the vicious cycle, but to forewarn you of this pitfall so that you will be better equipped to handle it when it comes along. There are many alternatives to "lashing out" at children when they try our patience.

Potentially abusive parents — those who have experienced abuse as children and are now concerned about repeating the pattern with their own children — can, with the right support, learn to break the cycle and provide a safe environment and positive discipline for their children.

Classes and books on parenting — as well as parenting support groups — can help you learn positive parenting skills to replace the abusive behavior you remember. But those special times of instantaneous reaction, those times when we really "lash out," need some extra attention. At those times, we want to remember to take a deep breath and reflect for a moment on what we are about to do. Make a list of praise-words — *positive* words about your child — and let that be your arsenal of equipment to reinforce *good* behavior. When you need to correct your child, use your praise-word list — tell him something good about himself. We naturally respond more positively to praise than we do to criticism! Criticism chiefly intimidates us without instilling in us the confidence that we can do better. Never pass up an opportunity to praise your child; use praise-words whenever his behavior shows even the slightest degree of improvement.

Jesus says, "Blessed are the peacemakers, for they will be called children of God" (Matthew 5:9). Peacemakers are those persons who avoid using violent words — who use words that build up instead of words that tear down. As St. Paul admonished the Ephesians, "Let no evil talk come out of your mouths, but only what is useful for building up" (Ephesians 4:9).

The American Catholic bishops tell us, "Within your family, when you shun violent words and actions and look for peaceful ways to resolve conflict, you become a voice for life, forming peacemakers for the next generation."[4]

Exploring our experience of childhood abuse with our "sculptor" will give us deeper insights into our own behavior and help us to understand our motivations: *Why* am I angry with my child? Am I really angry with him or am I displacing anger about something else on to him? Why do I react in this particular way to this particular behavior?

Before my son Anton was born I had isolated specific forms of treatment to which I had been subjected and which I definitely wanted to avoid communicating to him. One was the gratuitous use of deprecatory names such as "ugly" or "stupid." Instead I endeavored to praise him as much as possible.

Another form of negative treatment I determined to avoid was the use of drastic threats to prevent undesirable behavior. This compelled me to substitute more positive methods of discipline: to promise rewards for good behavior and to spell out the negative, *realistic* consequences of misbehavior.

Thomas Gordon, founder of Parent Effectiveness Training, cautions us to "be a person, not a 'parent.' "[5] He observes that when persons feel they have to become "different" and start acting like "parents," "unfortunately, this transformation makes people forget that they are still human — with faults, limitations, feelings, inconsistencies, and, above all, rights."[6] It is important that we let our children know we are human. It is also important that they know that we always love them, despite our limitations, despite our occasional angry feelings. If we strive to appear "perfect," if we always hold ourselves and the other parent to be above criticism, then we set up that arbitrary and false dichotomy between the perfect, omnipotent parents and the imperfect, helpless child. In chapter 2 I alluded to the possibility that the child being raised with such a dichotomy will have difficulty in identifying when he has reached the magical age of adulthood, with all the rights that pertain. Another possibility is that the child learns never to trust his own judgment of or intuition about other people. If he sees his mother behaving in a patently unjust fashion, and yet (a) his mother refuses to be reasoned with because she is "always right," or (b) his father refuses to listen to any criticism of the mother out of some misguided wish to put up a united front (or because he cannot accept that he hasn't married the "perfect" woman!), then the message the child gets is that his instinctive evaluation of his mother's behavior was erroneous. The child then concludes that any impression he forms of another person must be wrong; he comes to regard his judgments of other persons as valueless and thereby loses a prime opportunity to develop a valuable life skill.

When Anton was very young I told Peter that if Anton ever came to me with criticisms of him I intended to take them seriously and hear him out — and that I expected him, Peter, to do the same if Anton ever voiced criticisms of me to him. Assessing people, their strengths and weaknesses, is no different from all other relational skills in that it must be developed first within the family.

A further precaution I took against Anton's remaining the "eternal child" (another result of the false parent/child dichotomy) was to give him responsibilities suitable to his age; this included such things as home chores and, eventually, his own bank account.

I have been quite open with Anton about my background. It has been important for him to see that a victim of emotional child abuse need not "wallow in her victimhood" all her life but can break free and be healed. He can observe how I have grown as a person over the years with the help of my mentors, and thus realizes that a life of dull staticity need not await anyone as an adult. As theologian Mary Jo Weaver says, "You can sit mourning by the waters of Babylon forever, or you can compose a new song, a song with your own good parts of the past remembered in it." I have chosen to compose my own new song, one in which my son can join with me in a duet of liberation.

## Forgiveness: Proceed with Caution!

### What Forgiveness Is Not

Forgiveness does *not* mean telling the perpetrator, "It's all right, let's forget that this ever happened." Nor is it *repressing* what happened to us, sweeping it under the carpet, denying that it happened or pretending that it wasn't so bad.

Alice Miller urges us *not* to repress the past and emphasizes the evil that results from repression. Her chilling studies of infamous dictators such as Hitler, Stalin and Ceausescu reveal the uncanny connections between their abused childhoods and their careers as cruel despots: each of them denied and repressed the pain and horror of what had been done to them as

children, which in turn impelled them to inflict the
same horror on others so that they did not have to feel
their own pain.

> We are urged to honor our parents and never
> question them, whatever they have done. But
> when I realize that millions of people had to die
> so that Adolf Hitler could keep his repression in-
> tact,...then I have to say: we cannot point out
> these connections often enough or clearly enough
> so that the mindless production of evil can be
> made transparent.[7]

We must acknowledge and face the pain of the maltreatment we experienced. This is *recognition*. Then
we must allow ourselves to feel the anger that we
dared not feel at the time we were being abused.
This is *rage*. The Recognition and Rage stages —
what Miller calls "emotional access to the truth"[8] —
are essential before the process of healing can take
place and before we can forgive. Forgiveness cannot
be something we do arbitrarily because we feel it to
be "spiritually necessary" — it cannot be forced! Indeed, the Recognition stage has to stay with us, to
pass into the Memory stage, which will ensure that we
do not continue the abusive treatment with our own
children. Without recognition we cannot break the vicious cycle of abuse. If we are not able to perceive
the true nature of the mistreatment we received and
thus to condemn it, we will not recognize the same
evil when it presents itself to us as a potential means
of dealing with our own children. It was recognition

and then memory that helped me isolate those aspects of my mother's treatment of me that I strove to avoid in parenting Anton.

One more thing forgiveness is not: It is *not* unconditional or one-sided. As Alice Miller maintains, "A child can excuse its parents, if they in turn are prepared to recognize and admit to their failures."[9] The victim cannot offer forgiveness without some apology, remorse or reparation on the part of the abuser. Such "forgiveness" trivializes the wrong done by the (presumably more mature and responsible) parent to the helpless child.

### The Necessity of Forgiveness

Hannah Arendt writes of "irreversibility and the power to forgive."[10] Irreversibility means our inability to change the past or to annihilate what has been done to us. The one means of redemption from the predicament of irreversibility is the faculty of forgiving.

*Forgiveness is trying to understand the perpetrator's behavior.* Abusers are not born that way; they don't become that way in a vacuum; they are formed that way, wounded by parental mistreatment in their own family of origin.

When I was around eight years old my maternal grandfather came to stay with us, ostensibly for a two-week visit, but he ended up remaining for nearly two years. He was a humorless and demanding man who ate and drank voluminously, quite without regard either for my parents' limited income or for the fact that my parents had to give up their bedroom so that he could have a place to sleep in our small apartment. Deep frown lines radiating from the corners of his mouth revealed a man with little ability to see the bright side of life: he never had a good thing to say about anyone. If he heard me practicing the piano he was quick to criticize imperfections but never praised the good passages. If my four-year-old brother ran through the apartment playing cowboys and Indians, my grandfather would yell at him to be quiet. Not surprisingly, my parents had some difficulty in getting another family member to take him when their patience had run its course.

The impression I derived from my mother's occasional vignettes of her childhood was of parents who had had more children than they could cope with either financially or emotionally. She was the seventh of nine children. When she grew older she assumed much of the responsibility around the home and was unable to attend high school. Yet she apparently received no recognition or appreciation for her efforts; she often told me that when one of her parents went shopping they would return with a treat for all of the children except her — "Next time," she was promised, but that "next time" never came.

Understanding the sources of our parents' own wounds can help dispel the notion that they deliberately — with evil intent — devised their abusive behavior. This can be a factor working for our healing. It should not, however, be confused with *excusing* their behavior. No one can be excused from abusive behavior; each abused person is called to confront what happened to her and to embark on the journey of healing both for her own sake and for the sake of her children after her.

*Forgiveness is seeing the perpetrator through a wider lens than just in terms of the abuse she committed.*

My picture of my mother is balanced by the realization that most of my good qualities came from her. If I am creative; unafraid not to conform to conventional norms; if I am adventurous and love to travel; sensitive to nature — then it is because she had these qualities. It was her love of and ability with music that I inherited: she always sang in the church choir, helped develop my ability to sing in harmony and encouraged me to sing in choirs.

By viewing our abusers through a wider lens, we not only release them from the exclusive identity as "abuser," we also release ourselves from the "victim" role. This is the essence of forgiveness: to break the stranglehold whereby victim and abuser are forever locked together in their victim/perpetrator roles.

In her study of "resilient adults," Gina O'Connell Higgins[11] discovered that a major element in the resiliency of these adults who had been abused as children was that they had let go of the "victim" role. Releasing ourselves from our "victim" identity is another important factor in our healing process. Again, however, it does not mean forgetting. Healing and justice must go together: our healing must encompass our resolve never to be victimized again. Thus, rather than forget, we embark upon the Memory stage and let our memories become the foundation of a conversion experience. Through the conversion process thus empowered by memory, we move on from "victimhood" to a new identity and we resolve to break both vicious cycles: the cycle in which abused child becomes abused adult, and the cycle in which abused child becomes abusive adult.

# Notes

1. Miller, *Banished Knowledge,* p. 5.
2. *About Preventing Child Abuse,* A Scriptographic Booklet (S. Deerfield, MA: Channing L. Bete, 1989), p. 9.
3. *Follow the Way of Love,* p. 27.
4. Ibid., p. 10.
5. Thomas Gordon, *What Every Parent Should Know* (Chicago: National Committee to Prevent Child Abuse, 1975, 1987), p. 7.
6. Ibid.
7. Alice Miller, *Breaking Down the Wall of Silence* (New York: Meridian, 1993), p. 92.
8. Ibid., p. 143.
9. Ibid., p. 136.
10. Hannah Arendt, *The Human Condition* (Chicago: University of Chicago Press, 1958), pp. 236ff.
11. Gina O'Connell Higgins, *Resilient Adults: Overcoming a Cruel Past,* tape of a talk given in Boston, MA, Summer 1995.

# 5

# Meditations and Prayers

Awareness of God's presence in our lives is an indispensable "spiritual backpack item" on our healing journey. This chapter offers prayers and meditations from Scripture, grouped according to themes. Use them as you need. Some provide words with which you can address God; others are texts in which you may let God speak to you.

## God's Love, Your Goodness

The saying goes that "God doesn't make junk." The very first book of the Bible affirms the fundamental goodness of all creation — and that includes you!

> God saw everything that he had made, and indeed, it was very good. (Genesis 1:31)

When we have grown up with a low level of self-esteem we feel inadequate and unwilling to trust people who want to get close to us; we believe that "if they *really* knew me, they wouldn't like me." Trusting that we are loved unconditionally by a God who knows us through and through, we can begin to develop confidence that we are lovable to other people as well.

O Lord, you have searched me and known me,
You know when I sit down and when I rise up;
   you discern my thoughts from far away.
You search out my path and my lying down,
   and are acquainted with all my ways.
Even before a word is on my tongue,
   O Lord, you know it completely.
You hem me in, behind and before,
   and lay your hand upon me.
Such knowledge is too wonderful for me;
   it is so high that I cannot attain it.

Where can I go from your spirit?
   Or where can I flee from your presence?
If I ascend to heaven, you are there;
   if I descend into the Pit, you are there.
If I take the wings of the morning
   and settle at the farthest limits of the sea,
even there your hand shall lead me,
   and your right hand shall hold me fast.
If I say, "Surely the darkness shall cover me,
   and the light around me become night,"
even the darkness is not dark to you;
   the night is as bright as the day,
   for darkness is as light to you.

For it was you who formed my inward parts;
    you knit me together in my mother's womb.
I praise you, for I am fearfully and wonderfully
        made.
    Wonderful are your works;
that I know very well.
    My frame was not hidden from you,
when I was being made in secret,
    intricately woven in the depths of the earth.
Your eyes beheld my unformed substance.
In your book were written
    all the days that were formed for me,
    when none of them as yet existed.
How weighty to me are your thoughts, O God!
    How vast is the sum of them!
I try to count them — they are more than the
        sand;
    I come to the end — I am still with you. . . .

Search me, O God, and know my heart;
    test me and know my thoughts.
See if there is any wicked way in me,
    and lead me in the way everlasting.

(Psalm 139)

I began praying Psalm 103, about God's unbounded
love for me, at the suggestion of my "gifted sculptor"
Anthony. It changed my outlook on life.

Bless the Lord, O my soul,
   and all that is within me,
   bless his holy name.
Bless the Lord, O my soul,
   and do not forget all his benefits —
who forgives all your iniquity,
   who heals all your diseases,
who redeems your life from the Pit,
   who crowns you with steadfast love
     and mercy,
who satisfies you with good as long as you live
   so that your youth is renewed like the
     eagle's.

The Lord works vindication
   and justice for all who are oppressed.
He made known his ways to Moses,
   his acts to the people of Israel.
The Lord is merciful and gracious,
   slow to anger and abounding in steadfast
     love. . . .
. . . The steadfast love of the Lord is from everlasting to everlasting
   on those who fear him,
   and his righteousness to children's children,
to those who keep his covenant
   and remember to do his commandments.

The Lord has established his throne in the
     heavens,
   and his kingdom rules over all.

Bless the Lord, O you his angels,
   you mighty ones who do his bidding,
   obedient to his spoken word.
Bless the Lord, all his hosts,
   his ministers that do his will.
Bless the Lord, all his works,
   in all places of his dominion.
Bless the Lord, O my soul.

(Psalm 103:1–8, 17–22)

The picture we form of God in childhood is colored by our relationship with our parents. If we have been abused, that picture may well be negative. Read these words of St. Paul as if they were written to you personally, and know that God calls you to a relationship of love.

I pray that the God of our Lord Jesus Christ, the Father of glory, may give you a spirit of wisdom and revelation as you come to know him, so that, with the eyes of your heart enlightened, you may know what is the hope to which he has called you, what are the riches of his glorious inheritance among the saints, and what is the immeasurable greatness of his power for us who believe, according to the working of his great power. (Ephesians 1:17–19)

## The Lord Is Close

Abuse crushes the spirit. Poet Maya Angelou, raped as a child by a family friend, asserts that child abuse turns a child who knows nothing into a child who believes nothing. The following scripture passages show us that the Lord is always present to help restore our spirit and our faith.

The Lord is near to the brokenhearted,
    and saves those who are crushed in spirit.

(Psalm 34:18)

The Lord is faithful in all his words,
    and gracious in all his deeds.
The Lord upholds all who are falling,
    and raises up all who are bowed down.
The Lord is near to all who call on him,
    to all who call on him in truth.

(Psalm 145:13b–14, 18)

The salvation of the righteous is from the Lord;
    he is their refuge in the time of trouble.
The Lord helps them and rescues them;
    he rescues them from the wicked, and saves them,
    because they take refuge in him.

(Psalm 37:39–40)

To allow God to heal our wounds we must mourn them, and to mourn them we must acknowledge them. The psalms and the prophet Isaiah help us to do that while assuring us of God's never-failing presence.

My father and mother have forsaken me,
    but the Lord will take me up.

(Psalm 27:10)

Can a woman forget her nursing child,
    or show no compassion for the child of her womb?
Even these may forget,
    yet I will not forget you.

(Isaiah 49:15)

## God as Loving Parent

We cannot change our past; but we can heal our negative images of parenthood by meditating on God's role in our lives as a loving and protective parent.

With weeping they shall come,
    and with consolations I will lead them back,
I will let them walk by brooks of water,
    in a straight path in which they shall not stumble;
for I have become a father to Israel.

(Jeremiah 31:9)

When Israel was a child, I loved him....
...It was I who taught Ephraim to walk,
    I took them up in my arms....
I was to them like those

who lift infants to their cheeks.
I bent down to them and fed them.

(Hosea 11:1, 3, 4)

[Jesus said:] "...Do not keep striving for what you are to eat and what you are to drink, and do not keep worrying.... Your Father knows that you need [all these things.] Instead, strive for his kingdom, and these things will be given to you as well.

(Luke 12:29, 30, 31)

[Jesus said:] "Jerusalem, Jerusalem...! How often have I desired to gather your children together as a hen gathers her brood under her wings...!"

(Matthew 23:37)

## Vindication and Freedom

The Lord empowers us to move on from our mourning to new life!

The Lord is the everlasting God,
    the Creator of the ends of the earth....
He gives power to the faint,
    and strengthens the powerless....
...Those who wait for the Lord shall renew their
        strength,
    they shall mount up with wings like eagles,

they shall run and not be weary,
    they shall walk and not faint.

(Isaiah 40:28, 29, 31)

I waited patiently for the Lord;
    he inclined to me and heard my cry.
He drew me up from the desolate pit,
    out of the miry bog,
and set my feet upon a rock,
    making my steps secure.
He put a new song in my mouth,
    a song of praise to our God.
Many will see and fear,
    and put their trust in the Lord.
Happy are those who make
    the Lord their trust.

(Psalm 40:1–4a)

Abuse paralyzes us, but as we journey toward new life, the bonds of our past will be shattered. Jesus came "to challenge our belief that there is something intrinsically wrong with who we are."[1] He came to challenge our self-perception as worthless, and "to release us from the bondage of the inner power that keeps us in a negative state of mind."[2]

When Jesus came to Nazareth,... he went to the synagogue.... The scroll of the prophet Isaiah was given to him. He unrolled the scroll and found the place where it was written:

"The Spirit of the Lord is upon me,
  because he has anointed me
    to bring good news to the poor.

He has sent me to proclaim release to the
    captives
  and recovery of sight to the blind,
    to let the oppressed go free."

(Luke 4:16–18)

Do not fear, for you will not be ashamed;
  do not be discouraged, for you will not
    suffer disgrace;
for you will forget the shame of your
    youth. . . .
The Holy One of Israel is your Redeemer,
  the God of the whole earth he is called. . . .
My steadfast love shall not depart from you,
  and my covenant of peace shall not be
    removed,
says the Lord, who has compassion on you.

(Isaiah 54:4, 5, 10)

## Notes

1. Jack Walters, *Jesus Healer of Our Inner World* (New York: Crossroad Publishing Co., 1995), p. 27.
2. Ibid.

# 6

# Resources

- If you are hurting from the wounds of emotional abuse from your childhood,

- If you are a parent who wants to nurture and discipline your children in positive, non-abusive ways,

- If you are in a position (e.g. as a teacher) to detect child abuse and want more information,

- If you are in any way concerned with the prevention and healing of the emotional abuse of children,

this Resource Guide will help you. Please refer to it for a variety of useful materials.

## Hotline

Childhelp USA/IOF Foresters National Child Abuse Hotline (800-422-4453). Provides crisis counseling, child abuse reporting information, other information and referrals, 24 hours a day, seven days a week. For a hotline near you, see your telephone directory under "Social Services."

## Books and Pamphlets

The NCPCA (National Committee to Prevent Child Abuse) publishes educational materials that deal with a variety of topics, including parenting, child abuse and child abuse prevention. The materials are excellent for professionals, lay persons, students and children. To request a catalogue, contact:

> NCPCA Fulfillment Center
> 200 State Road
> South Deerfield, MA 01373
> (800-835-2671)

John Bradshaw. *Bradshaw On: The Family. A Revolutionary Way of Self-Discovery*. Deerfield Beach, FL: Health Communications, Inc., 1988.

Marla Brassard, Robert Germain, Stuart Hart, eds. *The Psychological Maltreatment of Children and Youth*. New York: Pergamon Press, 1986.

Diane D. Broadhurst, Marsha K. Salus. *Will You Speak for the Children? How Schools Can Respond to Child Maltreatment*. Hartford, CT: Children's Trust Fund, 1984.

James Garbarino, Gwen Gilliam. *Understanding Abusive Families*. Lexington, MA: Lexington Books, 1980.

James Garbarino, Edna Guttman, Janis Seeley. *The Psychologically Battered Child: Strategies for Identification, Assessment, and Intervention*. San Francisco: Jossey-Bass, 1986.

James Garbarino, Cynthia Schellenbach, Janet Sebes et al. *Troubled Youth, Troubled Families*. New York: Aldine de Gruyter, 1986.

Alice Miller. *Breaking Down the Wall of Silence: The Liberating Experience of Facing Painful Truth*. New York: Meridian, 1993.

Jack Walters. *Jesus Healer of Our Inner World*. New York: Crossroad Publishing Company, 1995.

David A. Wolfe. *Preventing Physical and Emotional Abuse of Children*. Offers practical techniques and strategies for early intervention and treatment for families at risk of physical and/or emotional child abuse. Available from The Guilford Press, 72 Spring Street, New York, NY 10012 (212-431-9800).

## Audiovisual

Clearinghouse on Child Abuse and Neglect Information, P.O. Box 1182, Washington, DC 20013 (703-385-7565) produces the *Child Abuse and Neglect and Family Violence Audiovisual Catalog* with descriptions of 500 videos, films, slides, multimedia packages and other audiovisual materials. Contact the Clearinghouse to purchase the catalog.

"Cypher in the Snow." 24-minute audiovisual, dramatizes psychological abuse. For purchase and rental information contact Brigham Young University, Audiovisual Services, 101 Fletcher Bldg., Provo, UT 84602 (801-378-4071).

"Hear Their Cries: Religious Responses to Child Abuse." Powerful 40-minute videotape, comes with Study Guide. Purchase or rent from the Center for the Prevention of Sexual and Domestic Violence, 1914 N. 34th Street, Ste. 105, Seattle, WA 98103 (206-634-1903).

"The Inner Voice in Child Abuse." 47-minute videotape (discussion tape also available), examines the link responsible for the repetition of physical and emotional child abuse from one generation to the next. Valuable for clinicians, parents, prospective parents. Purchase or rent from The Glendon Association, 2049 Century Park East, Ste. 3000, Los Angeles, CA 90067 (310-552-0431).

"Psychological Maltreatment of Children: Assault on the Psyche." 19-minute videotape by James Garbarino and John Merrow. For purchase and rental information contact Penn State University Audio Visual Services, Special Services Bldg., University Park, PA 16802 (814-865-6314).

"Some Scars Do Not Show." 10-minute audiovisual with child therapist Susan Linn and her puppets speaking to children. For purchase and

rental information contact Family Information
Systems, 69 Clinton Road, Brookline, MA 02146
(617-232-3737).

## Organizations and Programs

Center for Family Resources, 384 Clinton Street,
Hempstead, NY 11550 (516-489-3716). Promotes prevention strategies, maintains a clearinghouse of materials and programs for professionals.

Children of Alcoholics Foundation, P.O. Box 4185,
Grand Central Station, New York, NY 10163
(212-754-0656). Operates a helpline that provides
referrals to national and local self-help, counseling
groups, treatment agencies.

Children's Center for Child Protection, 3020 Children's Way, San Diego, CA 92123-4282 (619-576-
5803). A supportive, child and family-friendly environment providing services to prevent, diagnose,
and treat child abuse and family violence and conduct research and professional education.

Effectiveness Training, Inc., 531 Stevens Avenue,
Solana Beach, CA 92075 (619-481-8121). Parenting classes based on Dr. Thomas Gordon's
P.E.T. method. Contact for list of classes and
information about a home program.

International Society for the Prevention of Child
Abuse and Neglect, 1205 Oneida Street, Den-
ver, CO 80220 (303-321-3963), publishes *Child
Abuse and Neglect: The International Journal,*

and sponsors an international congress every two years.

NCPCA (National Committee to Prevent Child Abuse). See under "Books."

Parents Anonymous, 520 S. Lafayette Park Pl., Ste. 316, Los Angeles, CA 90045 (outside California: 800-421-0353; inside California, 213-388-6685). Self-help program for parents under stress and for abused children. Peer support in seeking positive alternatives to the abusive behavior in one's life.

Help for POST-ABORTION SYNDROME...

## A PATH TO HOPE for Parents of Aborted Children and Those Who Minister to Them
Rev. John J. Dillon     80 pp.     $5.95

*"Should be a required textbook for anyone who wants to be involved in post-abortion ministry."*
— VICKI THORN, Founder, Project Rachel

*"A gift for all who seek to be healers and reconcilers...a special grace for the hurting seeking the freedom of God's boundless love."*
— FR. JAMES P. LISANTE, Director,
Office of Family Ministry, Diocese of Rockville Centre

*"John Dillon understands the pain of aborted parents and gets right to where they are hurting. This is a wonderful how-to book."*
— SUSAN KLESZEWSKI, M.S.W., L.C.S.W.,
Psychotherapist

Available in Spanish:
**UN CAMINO HACIA LA ESPERANZA**     $5.95

# Published by Resurrection Press

| | | |
|---|---|---|
| A Rachel Rosary | *Larry Kupferman* | $3.95 |
| Catholic Is Wonderful | *Mitch Finley* | $4.95 |
| Common Bushes | *Kieran Kay* | $8.95 |
| Christian Marriage | *John & Therese Boucher* | $3.95 |
| The Gift of the Dove | *Joan M. Jones, PCPA* | $3.95 |
| Healing through the Mass | *Robert DeGrandis, SSJ* | $7.95 |
| Healing Your Grief | *Ruthann Williams, OP* | $7.95 |
| Let's Talk | *James P. Lisante* | $7.95 |
| A Path to Hope | *John Dillon* | $5.95 |
| Inwords | *Mary Kraemer, OSF* | $4.50 |
| The Healing of the Religious Life | *Faricy/Blackborow* | $6.95 |
| Transformed by Love | *Margaret Magdalen, CSMV* | $5.95 |
| Lights in the Darkness | *Ave Clark, O.P.* | $8.95 |
| Practicing the Prayer of Presence | *van Kaam/Muto* | $7.95 |
| 5-Minute Miracles | *Linda Schubert* | $3.95 |
| Faith Means... If You Pray for Rain, Bring an Umbrella | *Antoinette Bosco* | $3.50 |
| Stress and the Search for Happiness | *van Kaam/Muto* | $3.95 |
| Harnessing Stress | *van Kaam/Muto* | $3.95 |
| Healthy and Holy under Stress | *van Kaam/Muto* | $3.95 |
| Season of Promises | *Mitch Finley* | $4.50 |
| Season of New Beginnings | *Mitch Finley* | $4.50 |
| Stay with Us | *John Mullin, SJ* | $3.95 |
| Still Riding the Wind | *George Montague* | $7.95 |
| The Joy of Being a Catechist | *Gloria Durka* | $4.50 |

## Spirit-Life Audiocassette Collection

Hail Virgin Mother   *Robert Lauder*                              $6.95

Praying on Your Feet   *Robert Lauder*                          $6.95

Annulment: Healing-Hope-New Life   *Thomas Molloy*  $6.95

Life After Divorce   *Tom Hartman*                              $6.95

Path to Hope   *John Dillon*                                       $6.95

Thank You Lord!   *McGuire/DeAngelis*                        $8.95

Spirit Songs   *Jerry DeAngelis*                                   $9.95

Through It All   *Jerry DeAngelis*                                $9.95

Resurrection Press books and cassettes are available in your local religious bookstore. If you want to be on our mailing list for our up-to-date announcements, please write or phone:

Resurrection Press
P.O. Box 248, Williston Park, NY 11596
1-800-89 BOOKS